JESTER

Grace Marie Grafton

Hip Pocket Press Mission Statement

It is our belief that the arts are the embodiment of the soul of a culture, that the promotion of writers and artists is essential if our current culture, with its emphasis on television and provocative outcomes, is to have a chance to develop that inner voice and ear that express and listen to beauty. Toward that end, Hip Pocket Press will continue to search out and discover poets and writers whose voices can give us a clearer understanding of ourselves and of the culture which defines us.

Other Books from Hip Pocket Press

You Notice the Body: Gail Rudd Entrekin (poetry)
Terrain: Dan Bellm, Molly Fisk, Forrest Hamer (poetry)
A Common Ancestor: Marilee Richards (poetry)
Sierra Songs & Descants: Poetry & Prose of the Sierra: Gail Rudd Entrekin, Ed.
Truth Be Told: Tom Farber (epigrams)
Songs for a Teenage Nomad: Kim Culbertson (Young Adult fiction)
Yuba Flows: Kirsten Casey, Gary Cooke, Cheryl Dumesnil, Judy Halebsky, Iven Lourie & Scott Young; Gail Rudd Entrekin, Ed. (poetry)
The More Difficult Beauty: Molly Fisk (poetry)
Ex Vivo (Out of the Living Body): Kirsten Casey (poetry)
Even That Indigo: John Smith (poetry)
The Berkeley Poets Cooperative: A History of the Times: Charles Entrekin, Ed. (essays)

Web Publications

Canary, a Literary Journal of the Environmental Crisis; www.hippocketpress.org/canary.cfm
Sisyphus, Essays on Language, Culture & the Arts; www.hippocketpress.org/sisyphus.cfm

Jester

Grace Marie Grafton

Orinda, California
2013

Published by Hip Pocket Press
5 Del Mar Court
Orinda, CA 94563
www.hippocketpress.org

This edition was produced for on-demand distribution by lightningsource.com for Hip Pocket Press.

Typesetting: Wordsworth (wordsworthofmarin.com)
Cover art: Brianna Johnson Smeds
Cover design: Brook Design Group (brookdesign.com)
Photograph of author: Miriam Geer

Printed in the United States of America.

ISBN: 0-917658-40-X
978-0-917658-40-2

To Michael, my special harlequin

Acknowledgments

Thanks to the following journals where certain of these poems have appeared:

Advice — *CA Quarterly*
Background — *TalkingWriting* (under different title)
Change — *Theodate*
everything's witness and vigil — *Ambush Review*
Fifty Cent Moon — *Turning a Train of Thought Upside Down*, anthology
Flying home from… — *Sand Canyon Review*
I cannot bring a world quite round, Although I patch it as I can
— *Unroarean*
Living in the Guitar — *Indigo Rising*
The Nude Out West — *Hardpan*

Pandora
if the night is long, remember your unimportance
Vocabulary
Musician and Mother
— all in *Verse Wisconsin*

Circus
Anonymity
— Honorable Mention, *Sycamore Review* Wabash Prize

Author's Statement

The poems in this book illustrate the deep and persevering inspiration I feel when I read poems or view art that moves me. Through my years-long practice of meditating on the art of others, I've come to believe in a communal imagination.

As I read another person's poem, a phrase will shimmer; a kind of light begins to buzz in my head, my sight and sense of smell sharpen. If I honor the numinosity in the "found" words, my own words start to come. My response is not intended to "parse" or "interpret" the other poem — its music, message or moment — but to find what the phrase itself, just those few words, awakens in my own perception, or the way it triggers a new experience my imagination wants to create.

As regards art or sculpture, the "buzzing" moment will happen when a certain color or shape, or a sense of scene, or even an intuition about the attitude of the artist, stands out for me. I feel latched onto it, and words, or a sense of place or person or attitude, bloom in my mind. If I faithfully listen to what it wants to articulate, my poem results.

In order to honor this sense of communion, I credit, in this book, whatever source inspired me. If artwork, I identify it at the bottom of the page or, in the case of a poetry source, I quote the other poet's phrase as title or epigraph to my poem. This is not to send anyone on a time-wasting search after the quote or piece of art. It is to give the reader the (optional) opportunity to read the actual words that provided the trigger for my poem. Or, in the case of art, read the title of the artwork, which is often as inspiring to me as a line of poetry.

Mostly, I wish to respect the art of others, which has given me so much.

Contents

Improv'

Impersonation

Singing the Blues

Last Act

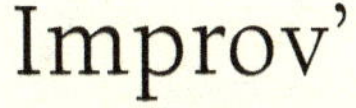

Improv'

Flying home from a lost wedding

The hasp of the chest flew open when it
landed in the spring-awakened field
two miles out of town near the willow-strewn
creek we remember catching frogs in.
The parachute bubbled down around it
but too late, the animal spirits had
escaped. The air around the chest, around
the parachute's silk, was in a dither,
worried that the music, too, would leak out,
which, of course, it did, slithering like some
slinky water creature heading for the creek
and, if it made it, the whole town
and all its environs would become *parade*.
The animal spirits would enter the bodies of
men who would feel compelled to drink
creek music. Soon the hare would be
honking the cornet, the deer squeezing
out accordion wheezes and the sax —
well, you remember the dromedary
has been waiting since that instrument's birth
to introduce to the world the Camel Rag.

title from poem by Rosmarie Waldrop

Improbable Improv'

At midnight, the deer deftly overstepped
the jardin's bounds, flicked jaunty
ears forth and back and —
in the universal language everyone is
required to subscribe to — asked the pawnbroker
what she'd give for this set of hooves.
That was just the beginning. The pawn
broker's tail fell like a waterfall and
slid off the edge of the green lawyer's tort.
It was a case worth arguing, the hooves
would emit a dazzling scent, like a heavenly
emissary in court, so the lawyer gave
the green thumb up and the pawnbroker
cribbed the deer down to four seasons
of leaves. To be left in the negative under
the troll's bridge. Indeed, the case
was about who stole the headlight
from the mayor's motorcycle, that night
they all climbed the reciprocal ladder
and everyone fell asleep in the detour.
Except the thief who averred he hit a deer
on the way to the mayor's house.
The hooves being the only part he
didn't recover.

to Wassily Kandinsky's painting "Improvisation 'Klamm'"

everything's witness and vigil

The parasol woman waits patiently
for sun's footprint to appear
on her apartment building's carnival
façade. Ambush of the expected.
Whose equilibrium woos cure for
the rainbow, shadowy co-conspirator.
Dancers hawk sweets under sunset marquees.

The trees don't know what they wait for but
their knees fill with water, their leaves
gossip with alacrity but know nothing
of ignorance and bliss, say nothing
that would reverse winter's revolution.

The man in the mustard-yellow vest waits
unquestioningly for evening's donkey
to amble towards him along Rain Road.
Answers and fertilizer, beads of the
bearable, where native bees build
nests in old leaves, buzz unforeseen
songs under surrendered matter.

title from a poem by Federico Garcia Lorca

The Last Saturday

On the last Saturday in May, she changed.
I suppose it was the moon, I suppose
it was the grasses that sprang up in their
enthusiasm and she couldn't say No.
They imprinted her newly-wrought fur
with patterns of sap. Insisted she shimmy
in the wind. She'd never been submissive
but now she meadowed into communal.
Threw her carefully carved profile into
mix and match. Her tongue became
sensitive as a snake's, leaves iridesced
in her sight, she arched her back to let
the moon scratch her spine. Yes, it was that kind
of affair. The town was scandalized, the priest
held up his crucifix and roared,
civic matrons clutched handkerchiefs
to their mouths, children were warned.
But she was gone. No longer vulnerable
to judgment. Above the creek's current,
prismatic shadows might be spied.

to D. Jack Solomon's painting "Last Look at Sheila"

Anonymity

Anonymity is what the moony man
in the forest most fears, that the trees' chorus
will green him out, leave but a husk
behind a trunk. No one's pang of regret
to spool into the memory: this was
his round face shining like a spoon
among bay leaves, above sword fern.
Wild roses wink, frogs croon not a syllable
of the tidy way his careful steps scissor through
the mossy bog, the sorrel carpet 'neath
redwoods' silent reach. He does not want
his life to masquerade as modesty.
Though quiet, he savors a sense of parade,
wraps his melancholy in an orange scarf,
brings a picnic lunch packed with
cherries and chicken, mustard, pickles.
His caprice is spicy, he sings arias
to waxy cap mushrooms, noses the understory
to find and admire piquant calypso orchids,
their polka-dot underlips and purple flared skirts.
And if he lies down on rocks beside the rain-
swelled creek, it's not to disappear but to wait
'til the shy, flame-bellied salamander
feels safe enough to wander near his hand.

to Tracey Heyes' sculpture, "Untitled"

Travelogue

He improvises a way, a world, a wooden map
to lead his career, how to crack the face
he thought he sought. Permanent
change unflags his country of origin.
He didn't think it would lead to dethronement
when he began to construct his ship,
he thought it was whimsy, farfetched
farther shore within a well-defined plot.
Where did the ancestors spring from, flouting
caution, defying safety to dare sojourn?
No frivolous venture, he starts to understand
as he rigs a barque with rudder (feeble
director) and patience becomes zeal.
He can't reconcile wish with affable
table-talk, he's starved to begin. Throw off
old ropes, light the blue lantern, touchstone,
learn to navigate by night, famished
for stars.

To Arthur Gonzalez' ceramic sculpture, "Travelogue"

Rocks

He does not like hair. The seriousness he inhabits
begs the sky for November rain, its persistent
erasure. Unsmiling and handsome, he offers refuge
to those who prefer to peer out from behind
bushes or rocks. The cliffs of Chinle where
native Americans continue to replicate the life
of their ancestors. A person could step
right into that canyon, to death, the drop-off
abrupt and implacable on the flat Utah plain.
So he refuses to allow the skin of his skull
to grow hair. When very young, he collected
rocks with his grandfather, who told him the old
stories of sky and the efficacy, as well as
judiciousness, of talons. Unadorned as his
grandfather's pate. The inevitability of the cony's
fate. He constructed edifices with the rocks
they carried back through mesquite and sage.
Each little structure carefully concealed
inner spaces a small animal might squirm into
and be momentarily safe.

to Georges Jeanclos' sculptures, "Head" and "Boat"

Advice

The mythical raven doesn't tell himself
"everything is going to be all right."
He drinks deeply of the dark,
until it comes out on his body,
clothes him through winter nights,
the Saturnian season, past all the bolstering
joy of solstice. He scoffs at those
delusional candles. Still, he
loves beauty, accepts on his slick feathers
the bluer stars' sheen,
raises an unruffled head on his thick neck,
turns and displays a sun-colored eye
which will tell you the truth,
which will sit you down and make you
listen sincerely to the worst-case scenario.
Not maliciously, but powerfully,
so you'll be prepared. He assumes
you can bear up under the brunt
of it, like him. Remember,
he changes the carrion he eats
into serious, purposeful flight.

to William Morris' sculpture, "Ravens on the Urn"

Portrait

Barely out of his monumental stage,
the marionette master imagines
a magical pony ride, without
the pony, without the magic, without
the day on which it would happen.
The nature of magic, interlaced with
shadow, dependent on foliage.
Thinking about the requisite
pony-ride-music brings on a fit of
shivers, teeth-chattering, spastic
movements of fingers and toes.
There is something akin
between the pony's mind and
his own. He's a bit afraid:
the tree is so green, the sky is so blue.
The pony's brown spots hover,
forming/dissolving as though
they were the years of his childhood,
whose portals he wishes never again
to enter. The pony's hoof-beats
provide percussion that
requires him to step, tip-tap,
in a dance which, board by board,
builds the stall he can finally nose into.

to Paul Signac's "Portrait of Felix Feneon"

Musician and Mother

Forgetting the date, the musician
steps into the purple, hard-lined morning.
He longs for the yellow gate, wants to remember
the way his mother laughed at rain, and
their trip to the puddle land. Before the war.
His dreams, his timpani, crash into
the red uniform landscape, lightning that skews
all plans. White towers, clean towels,
running water in every garret. He imagines,
even feels, the garrote slip tighter
around his gullet. Mother didn't last long,
he blames the rain, her unstaunched love
for wet grass. The tip-tap tappeta continues
in his mind, all the steps they stepped together,
her violeta dress, the way she swung
her beaded bag to the campanile's chimes.
Percussion of the streetcar. The escape route
requires the ladder-climb his mind relies on,
absent angel ascending, her click-clack,
tip-tap shoes drip on his fontanelle as he
follows her into clouds.

to Paul Klee's painting "The Musician"

Living in the guitar

The night orchestra's notes hide in the guitar's
innards, bickering over repertoire.
Over the guitar's hundred-year existence, they have
grown accustomed to stricture as well as liberation.
They know *plotz,* they know *soar.*

Made of fingers and the guts of cats,
they're formed from past and future chords.
When anyone (who hears in his head) plucks the strings,
their bickering elongates into more than wailing,
though sorrow and wishful torment tenderly underlie
the gilded glissando of the treble clef.

They're content to be ensconced in the instrument's core,
the wood, and the water within the wood.
The stintless passion of the hands that fashioned their domicile
swirls around them and provides them
with all the furniture they need.

to Kazimiera Kalkowski's ceramic sculpture, "Guitar"

As might be predicted

The stand-ins all stand in a row,
their wardrobe of interstellar art wordlessly swirls
in revelatory veils around their torsos
and into the erotica that liberates psyches.
Oh, radiator that warms and entertains the past,
that changes and reorganizes humanity's
unrepentant History which should — by all rights —
confess its overfed thorns and purposeful
woundings. Oh, Death that sucks down
all the dancing motes.

They drum their skinny drums in the midst of
the messiness they've created.
They celebrate the way their lips bulge into
beeline staccato. Tickling their audience
with unsummed arithmetic, they are prehistoric
in their argument against columnar edification —
indeed, against edifice of any kind.
They love to stick out their garlanded behinds,
they love to kiss the air until it's breathless
and willing.

To Roger Capron's ceramic sculpture, "Super Corte Maggiore"

Composite

It is no blue boat, sail·of sky, that takes her into
the imagined city. Nor the furled unnationed flag
that tempts her red/gold fingernails to betray her
to the occupying forces. It isn't the force concealed
in the egg wrapped incongruously in a broken-open
conch shell. She is next to the water wondering
which green could label it. The swallows won't
give her the true color though their swivelling flight
illustrates the truth. Take the red mountain, the half
she can see, adrift like her dream of skiing without
snow. Take the way the city's skyscrapers lead
her into the frisson of anything height could illuse.
Necessary, she decides, to accept lies or she'll miss
the purpose of the parade. The cat head and
the parrot fish seem to say, it's foolish to expect
books' pages to continue writing what they began.

to Barbara Rogers' painting, "Ecotone"

Mary Red Blue Green

She does not flinch from color.
Her paintbrush kindles benign and daemonic coherence.
She steps to what-comes, wearing combat slippers and boa.
She ornaments her ears with all-that-matters: Mother's silverware,
Grandma's brake job, the river. These cushion her disillusion.
Beyond newspaper and radio, the current scramble after fundamentals
and wishes that Overarching would take control,
she's stubborn. Primroses, bacon, galoshes ready by the door.
Her wall of augmentation allows her nightly out of self.
The wall gains weight.

to Toby Buonagurio's sculpture "Bionic Toby with Pet Boa"

Ribbons

He feels gold unfurl from the back
of his right arm. He uses it to counter
the black that builds a strict rectangle
around his hope for a future in which
he can marry. Red church, green beauty,
the room at the top of the stairs where
light floats in from four directions. Surely
gold will bloom and break out all black
angles; even the strictest father can
want a daughter. Orange ribbons a-flutter
in the sweep of his hair, flurry
in his throat. His bride's wide hips and
the glory of her belly. Bells make churchy
colors float out the door. He knows it's glad
love they celebrate, church constructed
by the gold in his shoulders. He lifts the
strict father who wears the black coat,
his golden shoulders bounce that father
like the little boy he once was. Together,
son and father make the curving yellow
cow that jumps one night into
the sky his hands reach for.

to Franz Marc's painting, "Small Composition"

Aspiration

He wants to roil his mother, never mind she's been
under the marble headstone for a whale of a time
before he finds his quarrel and begins to quibble
in a faster boil. First he spatters blue
paint on the living room she had nailed into
crème de vanille. Always the ice cream she
ordered, never dribbled a chocolate drop
on her crisp biddy blouse. Yes, he did, he
was a chocolate snarl on her lint-free
upholstery. Next, he dabbles in untangling
her jewelry collection, pearl redoubt, ruby flame,
that ring she discovered him wearing and
the subsequent trouble in his gender identification.
Even still, she was not flustered. But now,
the mis-setting of her dining room table, mixing
kitchenware with the Haviland, plastic
glasses next to the crystal, the droll
Christmas-creche figures garbling the message.
Gnarl in his heart slowly uncrimping.

to Augustus Vincent Tack's painting "Aspiration"

Purchase

The last item left at the auction where
up ‘til now he hasn’t committed himself
yet there is this wad of money impatient in his
pocket, it almost has voice, almost has
legs. He can’t shrug away its insistent
bray just behind his connoisseur’s mind.
He has a fateful sense that things must change.
The resemblance between this last, left item
and the first thing sold makes
his tongue tingle. He wonders about
the blue in the thing’s corner, wonders
if he could live with it. Might he not
bargain with his money, ask it
if it could be reconciled to his pocket
‘til the next auction? or perhaps achieve
satisfaction paying for the groceries — after all,
there are gourmet roasts of coffee, there are
imported cornichons and haute couture
almond paste. Everybody needs a kind of
meat to fortify the blood. Blood, very
different color from bleached-out blue.

to Helen Frankenthaler’s woodcut, “Cedar Hill, 11c”

He paints "The Sleep of Caliban"

He paints the picture of the tree ancient,
yellow bark, or brown or that
curious old-thing white.
Gouges of darkness in the bulk of the trunk,
indentations an animal could fit in,
in case of danger. Some branches dead,
spindly outcroppings from the outsize trunk,
ring upon ring of years, yet tree has
no memory. Living branches click
in wind, he paints the leaves as a blur
toward green, scattering to blue,
sky's reach he wishes to remember.
The aged sky. Then paints himself
asleep among red flowers that cling to
the trunk's base. And he dreams. He paints
his dream. His skin is brown, he is like a baby,
he is old, as old as the tree but not
as old as the sky. Butterflies talk
to him, their voices like the smell
of his mother's hair. He paints butterflies.

to Odilon Redon's painting, "The Sleep of Caliban"

The Jester offers his heart

There was an excavation into his use
of a pig to represent the heart that
cannot be resisted; there was an invest-
igation into his choice to assign
the pig angelic status; they all tried
to parse the meaning of his adopted
identity as a ram: object of the pig's amour.
Oh, the chaise they lay upon and how
to get the horns out of the upholstery.
The difference between their ears,
and the moral issue of species inter-
breeding, and the religious issue of
was this a female pig or a male because
clearly the goat was a he. And finally,
the consideration of appropriate artistic
expression. Debated long into the night,
January into February which they all
wished was not a foreshortened month,
all of them brimful of righteous opinion
and plenty of their host's best wine,
all of them altogether ready to be
entertained and titillated by the artist's
depiction of indiscriminate animal lust.

to Laurence Simon's ceramic sculpture
"An Angel Offers Me His Heart"

if the night is long, remember your unimportance

Everyone gathers for the rehearsal.
He is forced to wonder what his part is,
anxious now about his dribbling verbosity,
his dedicated need to peacock.
Equanimity has not been his hazard.
He loves costume, buckles in too-obvious places,
elocution pinned like a badge to his cravat.
How his longings mock him, how the sunset
truncates his would-be's. His best friends
won't allay his fears of anonymity,
they too vie for the mermaid role,
no one wants to be the bramble. "Oh me,"
he thinks, "how can I bear to be the wraith,"
who never makes it past sunrise, who hasn't
even a speaking role, cannot put a dent
in the action. How to make the best of it,
quell his fears: the loss of Mother's esteem?
The wraith's one strength is abundant time
to ruminate on self-improvement courses.

title from poem by W. S. Merwin

Sunday

It's in the day's birth that he comes to the red town —
red roofs, red doors and door frames,
he asks himself (beyond belief)
if finally the world has become as he knows it.
Everyone always laughing and indulging him
in his pink puffy pants, his Sunday clamor
about pink circles around the sun
and jocular women who can fly - how they
take him gliding into night's ribbons.
"And what color be those ribbons, my boy,
and did they whisper to you their daft recipes
for plum-crazy pie?" Still, the people always
like to hear his violin, they press upon him
raisin cake, they dance with him if they've
drunk enough of his grandma's berry wine.
And now look, if they were to come into the redness
of this new town, the blessed orange-haired
mother bending down with her paintbrushes and
crown, wouldn't they all shudder with wonder?
Wouldn't they toss away their shoes and ride
the small brown cart into the city center,
wouldn't they learn an entirely new tongue?

to Marc Chagall's painting "Red Roof"

the nation of shadow

The men work behind curtains,
the curtains lean against the waterfall,
the shadow woman in her pink straw hat
wears patchwork like a knife blade.
Now her aluminum bracelet yields its
bell tone the way her eyes understand
the ruined world the workmen repair,
combing and combing out
the inheritance of pain, shards
into the trough. As afternoon ends,
guitar strings on their pegs hang smiles
from the plaid curtains. The shadow woman
rolls in her secondhand piano, placid ghosts
from various addresses become the orchestra
with vacant demeanor. Yet there is no reproach,
what's provided is accepted, a basket
filled with immanence. The ghosts gather evidence
of partnership, doubt's put away, the door
behind the workers opens, ceiling
a belt of sky unbuckled.

title from a poem by W. S. Merwin

Pandora

Swarmed, a flash to the heart, she wants
to grab it back, wants to fan out with the forms:
be winged. And understands why she'd been
warned. Nothing would ever fit again.
Straight scattered into zigzag and myriad —
a fluvial harmony she's only, in dreams.
Her mother's wishes, Father's protection,
even her hiking boots and down vest,
she'll have to beg for them now. Oh honey honey,
blending skin to dazzle. Fecundity a fragmented
architecture, her body filled with fluff and too much
laughter. Sky, earth, animal legs, ears,
total voice, how can she hear them all,
now she's dedicated to float and flow into
every interstice, all the wrinkles in the elephant's hide,
dedicated for the rest of her life to find, to find.

to Mary Frances Judge's painting "Pandora"

The time for standing to one side is near

but not yet. Today she'll be right in
the middle, scrambling against all odds
to center stage, while still maintaining
her rhythm. She doesn't want to appear
rushed. She's wary of the palms' prickly
tips and the tropical humidity. Her coiffure
mustn't droop despite the damp.
It's true, she has the blues, they even
show up in her clothes, much as she
mulls the yellows and pinks. Dawn
and the blotting of night. She has always
thought in reverse, and considers thought
itself to be as ancient as the magnolia
trees that line the walkway through
the park by the river. Where the temporary
stage has been constructed. Where she'll
perform, as long as they don't expect
a sonata or roundelay or political speech.
How ruthless the public is, yet if she wishes
her reputation not to dwindle, she'll remember
the nature of all performance is despair.

Title from poem by John Ashbery

wild and fresh and thankful for any small event

What would have happened if,
long ago in the terrifying terrain of adolescence,
she had been Comet Dog
instead of Minxie Mink, desperate
under irresistible sable?
Comet Dog's courage, a flash
through dusky high school halls,
refulgent orb shimmering night and morn
among oaks along the river roads.
Comet Dog, vocalist par excellence,
dancer on the performance floor.
Who could have matched Dog's whirl,
her daring tutus, her embroidered cowboy boots?
Who could have known how deliciously
quiet she was under her spiky fur?
Who could have predicted her deep and steady
connection to Great Mother Dog,
how throughout her life, she would show
all those who cared to look
how to see Mother Dog's unwavering visage
in the sky, on the surface of water, in
mountains' rise, in the Aeolian croonings
around any eave of every home?

Title from poem by Rumi

Ritual

Comet Dog, incisors of silver
and legendary claws, subdues
the singular Beast who tries
to keep the fancy dancers
huddled into straight lines, one color
or one other. The ruse of Bull's Eye
released by Comet Dog's wand of
flame, scatters into fishes,
how many stamens and sexual touches?
When does flame not burn?
When does tooth not bite?
Comet Dog, elemental sage,
clacks the rattle of vast array.
Multi-spoked wheel never stops.

to Don Allison's painting, "Ritual"

The guests

Bearing in mind as she bares herself of garment,
weathervane and vernacular, she's chosen
to carry nothing today. In the strata of bedrock,
she innovates an ambivalent community.
For she is not alone, she is not naked alone,
she doesn't sit down to breakfast alone
or forlorn or eclipsed. Sits on the three-legged
stool painted seashell blue and shares out
the pie. Smaller and smaller portions as
more arrive. Loaves and fishes, feathers
scales hair fur hide. Hidden between
the boards of the table painted lip-service green,
excellent red and morning glory.
She is the supreme storyteller, is why
they all return eventually, although
many believed they could stick it out in
the realm of upholstery and automatic answers.
Intrepid traveller, she takes them far into
the arbor and the creek's riparian corridor
as she intricately fabricates constellations,
maple tree tassels, crickets' legs and
frogs' gifted tongues. They are grateful,
it's all free, she never charges admission.

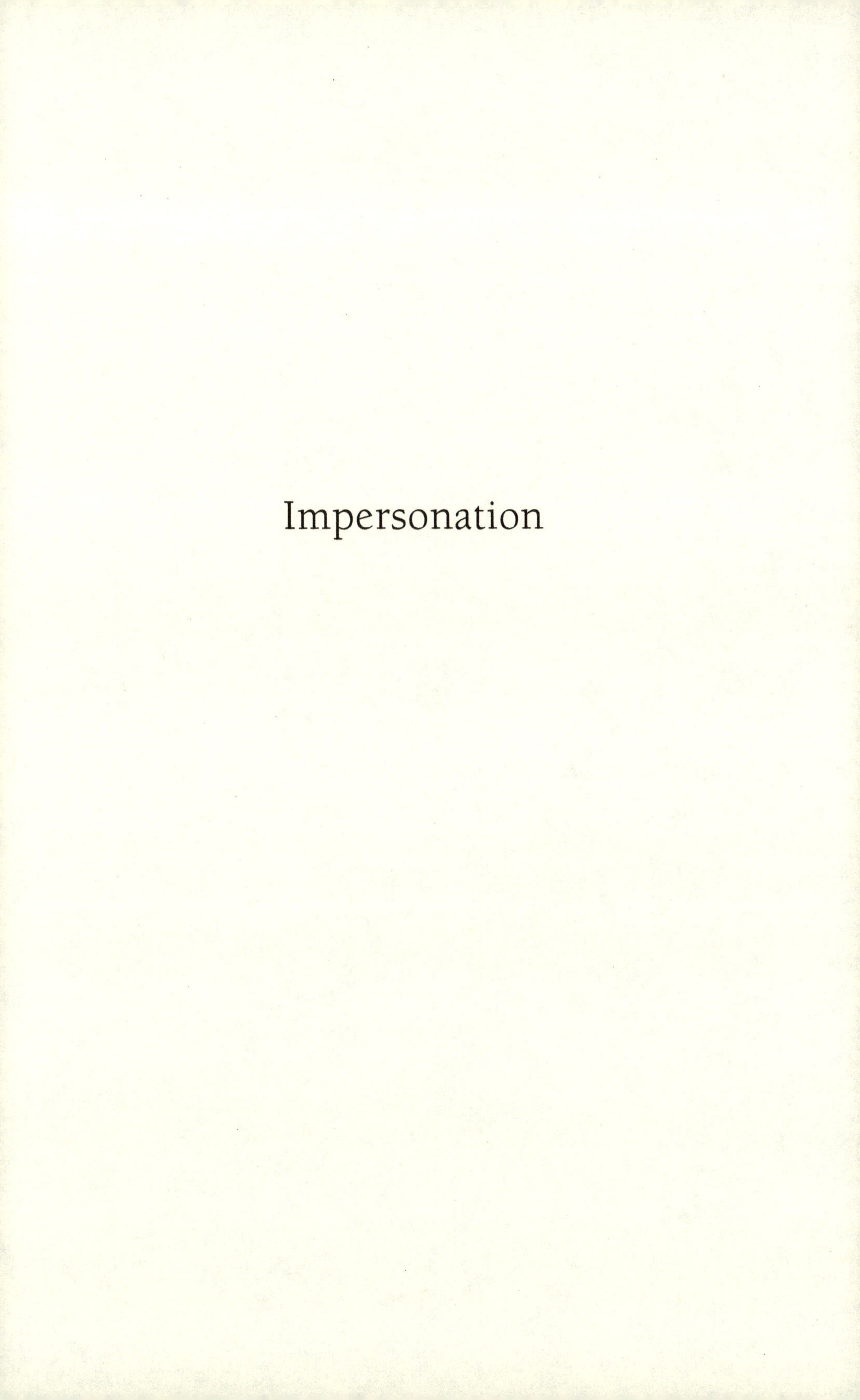

Impersonation

Luster

Who's gone and who's to come?
- Michael Palmer

Who scooted the red dish off the cliff? If
Mother hadn't strung that snare right there
hanging off the manzanita, dish would've
catapulted straight into the gorge,
and Mother's heart along with it. Dish
from Mother's friend Bertha, couldn't say it was
a dalliance (what's a daughter to know?),
but they were a matched set, Mum the spoon
to Bertha's fork. Worked together
in the five and dime. Now Bertha's dead
and the desert dish from San Antone is
the only souvenir from their dance down the aisles
of egg-beaters, penny balloons and hair nets.
All I can say is, catching that dish
instead of the doves she was after
'll have to do for dinner.

Folk tale

I began to be possessed by a wish to visit
the other village.
— W. S. Merwin

Listening, on Saturday night, to the lamp regale us
with light's vernacular, we enter a sumptuous
reverie, remembering that movies featuring
nineteenth century lawns console our apocalyptic fears.
Torrential rain, pulmonary edema, the raft's
inability to float. Grandpa with his noble
pronouncements: "I pray for a sudden death,
lightning strike or massive stroke, or to be
hit by a car while riding my bicycle.
What I fear most is torture."
He sat in his big chair under the wisteria arbor
and we listened to him sing under his breath
as he slowly died of Parkinson's. But there were
apricots when he was fifty and we were
six, flame-colored apricots that told us
stories of June from their perch in the tree
of spade-shaped leaves at the base of the bluff.
We picked them, they tasted warm from the sun.
There were no sloping lawns and we went barefoot.
Cousin Kenny swung the headless garter snake
around his head, trying to scare us girls but
we laughed and listened to the sun going down
and thought of Uncle Arnie whose toes and fingers
rotted off in the jungles of Bataan, he wrote
in letters to Aunt Frieda whose tears were torrential
even now because Uncle Arnie was tortured
in the war and never made it home.

the secrets I wore at my throat ....had come open

This is the heat that cajoles hyacinths
to confide their fragrance to April air.
Jostle of my hand against your hand.
Churn my will into love's cove, wedge my
too-serious wound against the iris
bulb's frivolous persistence. I'm just a
farce in the greatness of history's lunge.
Here's a step, here's a stepladder, bring it
around the side of the forest, my swath
of lost intentions, static, in need of
a breakdown or a rise up or a couch.
Believe me when I tell you I have no
oar to guide my soul's boat, I've never been
a good adventure, more Snow White's step-
mother, "Oh mirror, mirror," what spell to
utter, to maintain my lazy manner,
my do-not-hand-me-that-shovel crown?
I did not know when I consented to be true,
that you'd accept my webbed feet and claws.

title from poem by Federico Garcia Lorca

Background

Time that one seizes
and takes along with one is running through the holes
— John Ashbery

Shave off the feathers, stop wishing
for an innocent bar room, there'll always
be my youth, a permanent adjective.
Think of all the words I've misspelled
and now I've reverted to inverting
letters. The letters I wrote to
servicemen who carelessly left them
in the barracks when they went
into the jungles to sip the cup
of death. My seventeen-year-old
ignorance, thinking myself benevolent
and ravishing. I knew nothing of
humidity, fear, stinking sweat and
necessary, murderous rage.
Got off easy with my dancing,
with my jukebox interpretations.
All I really had then, all I really have now,
is my ability, in still moments,
to step back from the rim and ruminate,
to realize my dance is but a hunched shuffle
that transports me as far back as forward.

Approach

At any moment, the bell will ring,
time for *next* to befall. My friend says
we all know how to enter the fray
as ghosts, slipping by the bell. But I feel
all too present, *hurry up please*
it's time. A motif of wildflowers, "Look,"
I said, "they have owl's eyes above the white
belly." Transient, so we must declare
our affinity early: night bird, bird of prey
vibrating in dream time. I want what
I want but no longer will I cheat for it.
He said, "Maybe this is the last time."
To see the wildflowers, to travel west,
to search for lapis lazuli among desert
stones. And does no good to remember.
Just ghost, the froth of selves, I'd
rather let it drift like pollen. Say *aura*,
say *mask*, say "I do not have to breathe
this way today." Turn toward the north.
Oh Owl, do you hate the full moon?

for Melissa Kwasny

The Artist speaks to Friends and Strangers

Several me's fit the tennis shoes, a gift from my slightly tilted ego. It began when the flute went mute, that me lived in the delusion that couples are where it's at. She ended up bodiless, her remainder riding sidesaddle, just a head tied on behind what was left of Jesse James. Percussion of horses' hooves, not enough blood in her brain.

After I gave her up to her empty fate, I donned the blue robe, bent over backward to efface my red hair. Myths of temper and fall colors. Sweat lodges seemed they might be an answer. Chief's head dress, native wares. Couldn't hack the moccasins, needed a sturdier sole. Tenderfoot out West.

Please give me direction, make me a medicine bag. Drifting toward denouement. Even in the West, clouds gather and sage grows tone poems, blue, gray, green.

I continue to carry the man on my back, but at least I choose my own set of beads, follow the moose's trail uphill, I couldn't do that in high heels.

to Joyce Treiman's painting "Friends and Strangers"

Intrusion

There was mountain scenery to screen my monstrous truth,
where did I store the green and morning air?

My deformed hand, cracked brow, the scream along the skin.
All the satin will not wrap away the seepage.
It has broken through,

I have a pig's snout, a piggish appetite. My heart a warty
white growth always on the look-out for a dais.
I am the stepmother who only ever wanted everything.

I must don my piggish crown, I must hack off my hand.
Hawk my beastly body through the town. Relish the shock,
the recognition.

This poem does not add up to twenty one

I'm looking for a place to put
my head down, cover the nicks
on the cherry wood table. How to do
the up and down through hot, hot
July air, let go, drop into the river.
To remember December snow —
hibernation, a good hidey-hole.
How long must this go on?

Into the cracks within the stuffed-animal wall,
tiny wishes push investigative hairs,
to see what inspiration is there. Not much
but a modicum will do, continuing
the work of the secret soap, antidote
to tumbling down stairs. Overwhelming
desire to push back, cliff-drop.

We've only a moment, says the ancient
Aztec, Two-Rabbit Seven-Wind,
in his poem of the day, one day out of
his 17,250, speaking roughly, to ride
the currents of the mind, to wind up
on the other side of the crack I probed
on day 14,600 of my brief but lucky life.

Visitation, or: eye made out of silver.

Someone from the moon comes down to earth —
it has to be night —
dressed in antique ivory and
the family silver adorned with gilt.
Whose business is it?
but people are thirsty for gossip,
snuffling into concealing leaves
like busy black-crowned sparrows.
It would happen only in summer, wouldn't it?
The moon is cold but sunburns easily, so
in the night, somewhere in the Midwest,
the visitor wraps damp heat, a garnet's
secret glow, around her, a skin.
Surely original Ohioans knew
which August night it might be
and lie quietly under hardwoods along the river
where she would land and they could peek.

Singing the Blues

Transparent

Trapped in the nub of day, the woman
admits the inertia that accompanies rain.
Is where burrowing begins. She thinks,
"There's no end, there's been no end since birth."

Rung after rung, she climbed the ladder
down into her present body,
each rung more unconscious,
as though an angel stroked, hummed and wept
as it cradled her descent.
She argued with the angel
to release her from what she knew would be
echo, each lifetime's fallible promise.

But now she wishes for the sudden flush
into forgetting that always signals the new.
Futility subsumed by infant heartbeat,
five fingers that tingle with uniqueness
in their grooves, their singular ability
to insure, again, an unequivocal touch
on the repeated incarnations of Earth.

attended…by other angels

The whirr of first intentions, as audible above the radio
as her pet canary's ebullient song.
Nothing serene interrupts sumptuous purpose.
In the Mardi Gras parade where the sound of brass instruments
splashes into doorways and window frames, recedes
around color-corners only to recur to enforce the no-talking rule.
Conversation a bruised haze beyond the convent's walls.
She wants to be more popular
but the drive to silence ails her, she's so unlike a dog.
The clink wind makes against her winter wish,
enough percussion to flag her into a week's worth of yellow.
The canary, feathers' enchantment. She admits
she doesn't want to host its loud life.

title from poem by W. S. Merwin

The Nude Out West

Someone slipped her a naked photo of
herself, that rock above the pool, her late
adolescent rage and refusal to be
inducted into the Hall of Wallflowers.
Those days the smoking of cigarettes
was a Bite-me, that dive she took led her
to every intention of honesty, but
when she lifted her reputation from
Picasso and the other male me-firsts,
she flicked her ashes into confusion's
tinder box. No wonder Mom didn't mother
her, the Old West Lost World, Hollywood
her sugar-tit. It wasn't uncommon
that when most of her friends chose to
sell their costumes, she chose to travel.
She got as far as the Bosphorus but
the rabbit will out, even uncaged.
A fireplace and couch became
her cloister, for thirteen years she wept
about the time she'd wasted dressed in
black and white, then stood up and
taught herself to walk again.

to Joyce Treiman's painting "The Nude Out West"

The unraucous cynic, faced with cancer

Nothing benign grasps her jaw,
a diffusion of nurses thaws her illness
then wraps her in the halo she has long refused.
Yes, cowboy boots and formal demeanor
as haunt to the reckoning of order.
Ordure.
She sees under the pediments,
she knows the bones in the foot
and the shock value of ram's horns.
Nevertheless, she climbs.
Circumventing her emergence as a real fake,
she flicks her ash in the corolla of the rose
even as she rubs her body with its petals.

to Joyce Treiman's painting "The Smoker #21"

Animus

She buries him in his orange cloak,
he is her doll of meaning
and she means to use her rags and
sponges of color to revive him.
Share her ten-gallon cowboy hat,
use raw wood to warm his blood,
take him trailing ink and color pulp
down to the river with her,
sometimes dragged, sometimes clutched.
His shadow is bigger than both of them,
but somehow she manages to dress him,
blue and yellow and crooked shoes.
He leads the way though she,
the artificer, has replicas up her
pant leg. She leaves room for doubt.

to Joyce Treiman's painting "Leaden Echo"

The Deal

Open with cane and top hat,
white shoes, soft-shoe shuffle,
shuffle the deck, someone
's going to lose tonight,
gonna be the goat.

She didn't mind the goatee,
wore it herself on occasion,
rhythm she steps to
through lilac bushes and barn
she cannot remember, it wasn't
her lifetime, nevertheless the joker
in the hayloft taps the beat.

She'll keep him.
She's drawn the cards,
her fortune's the chair she sits in,
she dances on the seat
and plays the bones.

to Joyce Treiman's painting "The Deal"

The Story

The form of her left hand remains in the blue-
framed window. There's the apple blossom stick
she found on the walk down south. They say
sand stone holds wind — caress, whisper, history.
Weather lessons she used to listen for, buried
with all that the population wishes to erase.
Lines and demarcations fill in nothing,
but need became the cloud that pressed
behind her right shoulder. The mother
the father hunger that, when she tried to
feed it, stepped back as if afraid.
So her rose became tarnished.
The story focuses on the strength
of the stem, how even after all those years,
it retains green at its core.
She found the old mirror rescued from fire.
In the faint replica she fashioned
the dress she was born in.

to Jacqueline Gourevitch's painting "In Memoriam"

a moment of total darkness before you step through on the other side

She folds the sky down on leaves
that flinch under the lack of weight.
It's time. Coming around again to the parcel
that must be buried before the storm
washes her skirt, steals her hat.
She burrows into the crease that past history
has nailed between colors. She's brave.
Knows it will be cold, knows frost always
wants to chat and jangle its décor through
the measly insulation. Frost is beautiful but
its tread stings a track in the palm of her hand.
When the trap door can finally be lifted,
she'll limp over to the elm tree that
taught her how to store secret water
so frost couldn't close the awful bargain.
She wouldn't call the elm friendly but
they share the experience of a green candle.
That counts for a lot.

title from poem by Louis Jenkins

Refugee

Sits on the porch swing under the blue mosquito-
repellant fixture, in the daze darkness nightly
ropes her into, when her inborn eagerness
dwindles and she can't believe in the word *if*.
Only the way the cat perks its ears as though
wind, disheveling leaves, might be a mouthful.
The cat hoards instinct; all she can do is
braid rope into the memory of crossing
water, her father warning her not to trail
her fingers over the boat's edge. Up 'til then
she'd thought water was friendly, the frogs'
teeming taunts, flash of silver fish that fed her.
Up 'til then, she'd thought darkness a blanket
full of holes and the sun just hiding
behind it. What a prodigious loss
her mother was, is why even now, she
sits out waiting for the blue electricity
Father swears will protect her, to signal
Mother, "Here. Over here is our new home."

to Arthur Gonzalez' sculpture, "Travelogue"

End of the Line

On a rank Monday, her legs feel random,
what a weekend, late moon
augments her stray hour. This is not
an estival dinner plate unbroken.
Ophelia must again be at her orisons,
fluctuating between hope and shrink.
It seems she's misplaced an arm
somewhere in the sidereal hours
near Pluto which has never actually
been seen by the human eye, naked or
telescopic. Her life organized more
by random gravitational pull
than childhood's hopeful chest of drawers.
Head feels like an exploded TV
and she is wrapped in electrician's
tape. No use, no lights go on,
now she'll have to call back and demand
the guarantee.

to Neil Brownsword's ceramic sculpture,
"Feel So Down 'Cause You Haven't Made Out"

the search for the beloved is full of paradoxes

Such litter she leaves as she sweeps aside
the turpitude hiding under the hydrangea
bush her mother mistakenly hankered for.
Forensic searches for clues to the whereabouts
of answers, while her questions continue
to gouge out a trough in her attempts to
breathe. Tangent of truth, ripped scarf,
flickers from childhood and the enamel
camouflage of *meaning*. Expose the bitter,
better dance, her fashionable sandals will
initiate stubbed toes. She loves to whirl,
she hates to be dizzy, she poignantly under-
stands the risks of aerial display.
Pare down the text of *how-to's*, the older
she gets, the more time she spends curating
the art show for novitiates, show that continuously
topples the tower of bones, too ancient
to be held up by string.

title from line by J. Ruth Gendler

Ferment

Crouched omphalos guards Dragon Baby, ruby eye covered by lulled blue eyelid. Carrying a valise and a piquant stutter, the seer enters the nest. She remembers the way to the river even while the unseeable surrounds her. Sauntering through the temptations of tranquility, she's trained Houdini, she's lived forever and isn't tired. Into the concentrated geometry of core, little by lot she banters a vigil, squints ice-chips off the wing, splices a heart-beat under the scales. The rousing requires her to imagine *lift*. Deep in silence lies sound, her veil locates flight. She blows. Shudder reverberates. The cube cannot hold, even mythology's dicta of beauty can't coax her surrender. Blunt jubilation escapes stillness, red raises its eyelids. Her hand wangles a way, river comes pouring out. Dragon must fly or be drowned.

to Brent Kee Young's sculpture "Turning point…Floating"

Found materials

Mocking loss, she collects what flood has strewn. A kind of baseline faith she rolls on, like Buddhist monks with their food bowls but who's in the habit of giving now? Still, minutes tick unmeasured, she picks and turns — painted board here, laceless shoe, strip of muddied table linen she tucks into her wheeled basket, fashioned of stuff she gleaned and nailed. Haphazard, mismatched, workable, each part from a past. She doesn't just follow the flood, she haunts backyard trash bins, patrols the dumps. People's lives teetering at the edge then leaving for Alaska, or the coffeepot and discarded TV because family fortunes rose and *better* wove its spell. She bets on the salvagability of tossed or partly burned, a ring of keys she jingles percussively as afternoon unlocks.

to Floyd Gompf's sculpture "Red Wheel"

How to untitle herself

She wants to be a hieroglyph, filled with history
and too mysterious to understand. It will take
days, each day she'll wear a different dress, first
the pink with the poofy bodice and form-fit midriff.
Assume an angular pose such as a snowy egret
forgetting how strikingly awkward elbows and
knees could be. Though she hasn't a beaky nose
nor pinpoint eye. But that white headfeather,
rising drifting, ethereal as a beautiful woman
is supposed to be. How form, in an historical setting,
comes to define meaning. And so she rejects
the idea that she means anything. A form of drift
in the midst of her era. What era is that?
Look intently at the second dress
she wears: dark blue silk sheath, here and there
a nub of thread seeming to indicate, within the
tasteful sheen, that even the best beauty is im-
perfect. Her unbeaky nose, the fact that she prefers
flats to high heels and drives a car, as the mechanic
says, "like a strong man." Certain things she doesn't
hesitate about, other things she holds back on 'til
her chance disappears. Adorning the dark blue dress
is a dark blue lace collar, the whole dress
much too hot. She can't wait to take it off.

to Elmer Bischoff's, "Painting #10"

To let it go

Deepening into decades, the desire to be a clock
adorns her hours with the entitlement she believes
dignifies identity. Indeed,
a secret sense of virtue is frequent —
her self-assessment, in all candor, more
compliment than genuine gesture.
She entertains herself,
especially through the summer months,
by scrutinizing the way the minute hand
seems to dance forward, grasping light
that pours increase from the verges of day.
It becomes her habit to confess, to this
most objective of listeners, her brazen wish
to attain to the same glorious indifference
the clock will never escape.

For Roy de Forest and Elmer Bischoff

The pervading alchemist — she whose subtle
fears propel a shuffle past the monsters
of integrity — accrues a paraphernalia
which undomesticates her formula.
She enlists doubt to be her Cerberus.
She invites her dancing shoes to counsel her
regarding the looseness in her overhead
illumination. She sinks deeper,
colors gain weight, a cobalt
sash, a burgundian tunnel, jet-black
expression. She can still see her hands,
glowing with a phosphorescent modifier,
they're like doves in a Giotto fresco.
She understands, there's no way out
of this spiral — as the child said yesterday,
the fish is dead and dead it will always be.
The natives taught the pilgrims to plant
a fish with the corn. It isn't an answer,
not even a hope, she long ago eschewed
those earrings. But can it be a practice?

Paper Hat

The hour midway into her life when she
sits down in the square chair inherited
from an indolent ancestor and remembers
what she meant when she made the paper hat.

Her grandmother taught her
to measure ingredients by sight.

Nothing bad brought her here,
no car, no vineyard truck, no ambition.
Her children weren't urging her.
The paper hat was an argue charm.
Sometimes it covered her eyes,
when she looked inside it was yellow or brown.

She didn't paint the hat but fashioned it
from leftover wallpaper scraps before the glue
went on the wall. She's lucky that way.

And the chair ending up on the back porch,
that's lucky too. She enjoys the wood
under her tailbone.
Her fingers curl around the pole,
her hat sits lightly.

to Hermann Muys' sculpture, "Paper Hat"

I cannot bring a world quite round, Although I patch it as I can

She lends him one long hair from the many on her head.
Token to dispel what he thinks is his workday.

This is before everything turns grey and the river
is diverted into a viaduct that runs
between altered fields.

She understands the meaning of the mill
with its great grinding he must attend.

Life is no longer reverie. Still, she lends him
her long brown hair before it turns grey.
He tucks it under his shirt.

Before the day becomes a grind and he's
covered by alteration's veil.

To dispel the notion that dawn is a trap
to draw them into the viaduct at the place
where frogs are swept away.

At sunset, he returns. She draws the long hair
from the sweat on his chest and leads him

by the length of it upriver, viaduct and mill left behind,
into the smell of what men haven't planted:
violets, mugwort, horsetail fern.

title from poem by Wallace Stevens

Not choosing

She steps to the canvas not expecting the ocotillo vine,
the pickled fire, these moments alone with her baby.

She leaves the dogs behind when she walks in woods,
hates rabbit blood on her boots, slobbered tangle of fur.

She chooses to keep only plants for pets but makes
the man's hair explosive to remind her of threat.

She thinks his medals for courage hide hatred, something
mundane mixes the exotic sock with the face of Jesus.

Her hair untroubled by any comb, she admits box canyons,
Nevada desert barren 'til she kneels right down to ground.

to Meinrad Craighead's painting
"Journey with Tortuga and Storm Petrels"

Change

On Sunday, she clasps the mimosa branches
in her fists, whirls them shake shake shake
over the garden bed where Mother planted cinquefoil.
Tiny yellow petals salt down on white flowerettes
so like the blossoms of strawberries, so like their
leaves. Unclips her hair, wants it frouseled,
churlish, as unkempt as mimosa's attempt
at unwinding winter's tight order. Cymbal crash,
cat ready to pounce. She chooses not to speak
the mother tongue but cashes in on the curve
of change like an existentialist. Carries
her dripping bouquet down the corridor,
a chorister of disorder, a Carmen
among coriander. She eschews slippers,
wants a warmer climate, cool tile
floor a welcome mat to lie on come
heated afternoons. Arranges the fleurs
in a complicated vase, whispers secrets
into all the nodding stamens, pulls out
her magnifying glass, looks closely into
the heady central location bees go crazy for.

to Pierre Bonnard's painting "Bouquet of Mimosa"

Tutor

What was that purple month, with spontaneous
bees over the wisteria? Grandmother's
frolic experiment, stealth corridor
grandchild had to traverse to reach
the back door, prolific beauty.
What's the hub around which equilibrium
forsakes caution? Teakettle undulates
in the boil, even air becomes a novice,
kitchen rite, totem breath.
Elation of quiet, the way the woman,
not yet old, enthralls the child in
wisteria's locus and the blossoms
of crabapple. Hands magnetize *hold* and
carry, brown hair a tutor. How could
petals and breath conspire to birth
the marvel of words from wordlessness?

to Pierre Bonnard's painting "La Petit Dejeuner"

Last Act

The invisible animals

Their cadence irregular, like a graveled hillside.
Did we ostracize them, we big-brained humans,
so in love with our *I-knows* that we detached
our hearts and hung them on the thorns?
Did our self-absorbed rejection germinate
their fear, their retreat into thatches and
curtained caves? Do we remember them at all?
Saying, over and over, our rosaries of loss. If so,
would these mantras restore to us a semblance
of the intact world? The one where we began,
before weather maimed us, while the nebulae
gathered and we were just particles, along with
the invisible animals who might have been visible
then but there were no naked eyes, no eyes at all,
no *I's*. Everything existed, everything was marginal,
our hubristic brains not yet a tuft of primal matter,
our language adrift. Whatever of us was to congeal
still invisible.

title from poem by Melissa Kwasny

we are all on loan

Douse the lantern, maybe they won't come
to take us back, place us in the green closet
or, greenly, enclose us where there's no air.
Or, if air, it's grainy, textured and if we turn,
we bump. Do we live in a mirage of freedom?
This cloak of body an alias, amalgam
of embellish and haunt? There are those
who believe in ghosts, are ghosts actually
escaped wishes, the longing to be more than
a promise? A promissory note? Musical perhaps,
which, as long as it can last, is allowed
to remain, like Scheherazade. One hundred and one
tales, one hundred and one nights we can
afford to ignite the flame, burn the candle,
paint the mosaic of breath, heartbeat, owl hoot.
Name the stars as we lie on the summer lawn
with our loaned children and the facsimile
dog. We've waited long enough after the illusory
sunset that the mosquitos have disappeared
into the trees' canopy. We almost feel real.

title from poem by Melissa Kwasny

Voice without throat, dark voice

Begin to bury the soaked letters.
They've diagrammed their last syllable.
Skeletal profile over there in the corner
behind the ideals, they're disappearing
with that final rubbery squeak.
To weep is allowed, it just must be
one of the new sounds, lyre plucked and
tuned as if we've never heard it before.
A sense of fire. A feeling of idiocy.
Mapless, many brooms sweep out
dried petals of last spring's anemones.
We don't know what to call them
but are dazzled by how they
hold color — red, blue, the intense black
that will provide the language seeds mean.

title from poem by Federico Garcia Lorca

Fifty cent moon

The fifty-cent moon exhilarates the night walkers,
who are foolishly searching for color.
Will silver do? No, longing impels them
to pursue the minute hand into the hours.
Before dawn, the rooster's tail begins
to exalt the rusty eminence it has been
given to crow about. Glory be! The walker's soles
are sore, their backs near collapse, they
prostrate themselves on rocks and let light swirl
a rainbow around them. These foolish pilgrims
have found their religion. They vow to become
the Johnny Appleseeds of floral largesse. Along
highways, in trashy vacant lots, down wild
watersheds, in parks where state budgets
can no longer pay for weeding, they strew seed
and bury bulbs — poppies, larkspur, Indian paintbrush,
mariposa tulips, douglas iris, wild pea.
At regular intervals, they deviously return
with their three-wheeled water tank, insuring
the seeds are fed. The water hose sprays
drops that marry sunrays to produce the prism.
Pilgrims' reward.

to Joan Miro's painting "The Red Sun"

The Yellow Town

The beginning of sunlight gathers boards
into planes and angles. They speak and nod
to moved air; waking birds are given
invitations to perch and watch and wash
in light. Yellow king, ochre queen
don work clothes, become the painters of day.
Newness, having drunk its fill of dew
and stillness, having wrapped itself in dark
and come to necessary decisions, steps forth,
at first as quiet as a pool. Building strength,
it lifts the houses, leaves and paths into
a heady thrum. Anticipation, tongues, shift.
The king and queen are carried on the shoulders
of the town, roofs and cupolas, steeples
raise them, laughing, into high air.

to Paul Klee's painting "Affected Place"

past asking the gods to please give back our keys

On the second day, understanding as she does
that she, among others (all others?), is indeed
the world's fool, she says "What the heck" and
finishes off the glaze by finger-wiping the shape
of an iris and its supplicant leaves into the goo.
Meaning both her surrender to the facts and
her flake of hope. Or is it her scribble of defiance?
This flower in Eliot's cruelest month, as year
after year she slips another vial of 365 drops into
her storehouse. So she makes vases, she glazes
plates, knowing she is snared in the everyday,
knowing she's fashioning earth into a thing
that will go back into earth. Her designee.

title from poem by Melissa Kwasny

Maids' afternoon off

This is when they start out for the orange cliffs
above the wily sea of light. Agreeing about
the particular dazzle such rusty orange kindles,
how they both want shoes that color,
how they wish to dangle on ropes down
the steep rock drop, above dangerous water —
arbiter of all that comes and goes — audible now
in its everlasting task. They want to risk
coming near the monster, then escape,
flinging their orange-shod feet into the nefarious
air. Pretend to be swallows that swoop and curve
and penetrate the cliff's impassive face. But
to drift down that way - swing-seats like they've
seen in the children's garden at the big house
where they work — would require engineering
beyond their ken. A couple of very strong men.
Their adventure eludes them. But the lavender
bushes, the wild-berry vines white-blossomed,
the bees and the near-green light. Someone, or
many someones, before them made this path
out into the babble above the sea. It's as though,
in the bees' drone, they hear the old ones hum.

to Claude Monet's painting "On the cliffs, Dieppe"

Vocabulary

remote as the glittering trash of heaven
—John Ashbery

In the bar room of adjectives sit the shaven
languages inquiring solemnly about their
barracks. Where to rest their syllables in
safety and benevolence? Alas, they sip
the poisonous cup, delude themselves into
believing the spectacle of omniscience.
License to practice *meaning*. Clearly
they have failed to study history, or even
everyday humanity's blizzard of incom-
municado. To learn *meaning*'s permeability.
The story of leaves' disintegration,
assisted by microbial mouths and incessant
weather, the jukebox of eternity. Nevertheless,
they help us ruminate on possibility and
potential, so long as we remain aware
that their shoes get scuffed and their hair
ascends into a place past communication's comb.

… go back where everything is nothing

He says, "Let us have nothing new."
She says, "You have no reason. There is
no new." He says, "Everything is new."
"In the sense of 'again'," comes her reply.
"Riddles," he says. "A very old game,"
she adds. "The transient truth,"
he observes. "A palace thief," she
concurs. Both of them look into
the trees (which have not spoken)
and recognize how the span of the day
(each day) encompasses and cradles
trees' imperceptible reach and stretch.
Do they believe in the trees' eventual
death, if they don't live to see it?

title from poem by Rumi

Circus

The moment when he discovered he liked chickens,
the moment when the woman in her floral dress
became the diadem on the horse's back,
the circus moment, embrace moment, the owl
turning its head 180 degrees,
the astounded moment.

She practiced slipping down the underside
of the horse, horse practiced equanimity,
there was rehearsal and jest between
them, she as acrobatic as a feather
escaping from a gyre, the horse's
face was green with envy, her floral dress was
a lofty impediment. She liked best when her head
hung down. The moment she discovered
how attractive were the horse's knees.
There was some danger.

The villagers mocked his love of chickens,
especially the red ones, the red and purple,
black-collared banty roosters, hens with a flock of
russet progeny. The moment when the horse's mane
looks blue, moment in the sky.

to Marc Chagall's painting, "Circus (Circus Rider)"

Grace Marie Grafton is the author of five previous collections of poetry. *Zero* won the 2000 Poetic Matrix Press chapbook contest. *Visiting Sisters* is a collection inspired by the artwork of contemporary women. *Other Clues* consists of experimental prose poems. A chapbook, *Chrysanthemum Oratorio,* plays with language and concept. *Whimsy, Reticence & Laud,* also from Poetic Matrix Press, explores the sonnet form.

Ms. Grafton taught for many years in the California Poets In The Schools program, for which she was awarded twelve California Arts Council grants. She was named Teacher of the Year by the River of Words annual student poetry contest co-sponsored by Robert Hass, United States Poet Laureate.

Born and raised in California's San Joaquin Valley, she lives in Oakland with her husband, Michael, and their extended family.

www.ingramcontent.com/pod-product-compliance
Lightning Source LLC
LaVergne TN
LVHW051015080826
845145LV00009B/2643

* 9 7 8 0 9 1 7 6 5 8 4 0 2 *